Navigating your finances God's way

Managing your finances according to the Bible

Peter J. Briscoe

Adapted by Mark Lloydbottom

info@yourmoneycounts.org.uk   www.yourmoneycounts.org.uk
 YourMoneyCountsUK   @YMC_UK

Published by Your Money Counts, UK. This course "Navigating Your Finaces God's Way" is a Compass publication.

Author: Peter J. Briscoe

This version adapted by Mark Lloydbottom in collaboration with the author.

Compass © 2017 compass@compasseuropartners.eu

Unless otherwise noted, Scripture quotations are from the Holy Bible:

The Holy Bible, New International Version®, NIV® Copyright © 1973, 1978, 1984, 2011 by Biblica, Inc.®
Used by permission. All rights reserved worldwide.

The Stewardship Studies in each Extra Time are included with permission from Christian Stewardship Network.

ISBN: 978-1-908423-18-4

Printed in the United Kingdom
Version 2018/3

Design: Dickie Dwyer

Layout: Loulita Gill

www.yourmoneycounts.org.uk

Welcome

Welcome to **Navigating Your Finances God's Way** - a course during which participants are taken on a journey of learning to discover what the Bible teaches about 'true financial freedom.'

Your Money Counts is a UK based charity and is part of the global family of ministries that are related to **Compass** and **Howard Dayton**, the co-founder of Crown Financial Ministries and Compass USA.

OUR MISSION IS:

To see every believer worldwide faithfully living by God's financial principles in every area of their daily lives.

OUR VISION IS:

To equip followers of Jesus in every nation to learn, apply and teach God's financial principles, so that they may know Christ more intimately, be free to serve Him and to finance the Great Commission.

That it is of vital importance to each believer to discover what the Bible has to say about handling money becomes evident from two very strongly worded statements in Scripture. "The love for money is a root of all evil!" (1 Timothy 6:12) and "You cannot serve both God and Money" (Matthew 6:24).

That faithfulness in our financial management is so important is also emphasised by the words of Jesus to his disciples, "So if you have not been trustworthy in handling worldly wealth, who will trust you with true riches?" (Luke 16:11).

The Bible is our guide in this course. Jesus made a wonderful promise, "If you hold to my teaching, you are really my disciples. Then you will know the truth, and the truth will set you free" (John 8:32). True financial freedom comes from learning the truth about what the Bible has to say about handling money!

Did you know that the Bible talks about possessions and money in over 2350 verses? Financial freedom is not so much a destination to be reached, but a process of getting our lifestyle and attitudes about money so that they are aligned with God's plans and bring His wisdom into practice.

Your Money Counts seeks to contribute to the work of the Church in "making disciples in all nations", specifically in the area of becoming faithful in managing all God has entrusted to us – good stewardship. Financial freedom means to be fully free to serve God and your neighbour. Financial freedom means not being weighed down with financial burdens that restrict our ability to be free - free to serve. Who, you may ask? Our families, our church, the unsaved - however the Lord leads.

THE COURSE STRUCTURE

The course comprises an introductory Module followed by five in-depth Modules. Each Module follows the same structure; two topics and a practical application. However, you are not required to disclose any personal financial information.

First, we go to the Bible to see what God has to say about each topic. Then, there is a short discussion period before going on to the next topic. The practical application session gives some exercises to put the biblical principles into practice.

In each Module we provide suggested reading from **Bought** which will provide further insight into your study of biblical finance. This workbook is an insightful resource which looks at many areas not included in this course. We also recommend that you learn a Bible verse to accompany each Module.

We thank you for your commitment to go through this course – attending all five Modules will ensure that you maximise the advantage you will gain as you uncover more of the wonder of God's Word.

The Bible has much to say about our MPG -Money, Possessions and Giving -so let's embark on the journey.

NAVIGATING THE COURSE

The first two Modules look at the blueprint for living financially while the next three look at what the Bible has to say about debt, giving and saving, investing and spending.

You will become familiar with the structure of the course and the features which are indicated with the following icons:

LET'S TALK

Each Module includes suggestions for discussion among the group.

TIME TO WATCH A SHORT FILM

Each Module includes films, some of them visit the coffee shop conversations – maybe there is time for your group to continue the discussions.

EXTRA TIME

You may find that the Module more than occupies the time you have. So, if you wish to continue your studying you have some 'extra time' activities. These include:

JOIN US AT THE COFFEE SHOP

You will find a range of videos covering a wide range of subjects.

STEWARDSHIP STUDIES: BIBLICAL INSIGHTS

Each Extra Time Module includes a study on Stewardship as this so lies at the heart of grasping the truths on what God wants us to know about our understanding and attitude toward money and possessions.

GOING DEEPER

An opportunity to delve more deeply into our Maker's handbook for life.

YOUR THOUGHTS, REFLECTIONS, COMMITMENTS AND ACTIONS

A personal record of what you have learnt.

SCRIPTURE MEMORY VERSE

Each Module includes a suggested Scripture memory verse. Jesus quoted the Old Testament frequently in his life and ministry. He quoted from 24 different books roughly 180 times! It is clear that he thought of the Scriptures as the ultimate authority in life and a way to understand the heart and desires of God. Why would we not follow Jesus by knowing and trusting Scripture the way he did?

We are called to memorise Scripture. Paul in Colossians 3:16 tells us to "let the word of Christ dwell in us richly." We must know Scripture first before we can teach it or apply as God desires.

The Bible says this about itself in Hebrews 4:12 "For the word of God is alive and active. Sharper than any double-edged sword, it penetrates even to dividing soul and spirit, joints and marrow; it judges the thoughts and attitudes of the heart."

You will find a page of all the Scripture memory verses in a few pages. This you may wish to cut out to facilitate your learning. The memory verse is repeated at the beginning of each Module.

BOUGHT

If you do not have a copy of Bought this can be ordered from Amazon.

Table
of contents

This course is designed to engage Christians in discussion to discover what it means to be stewards or managers of the assets that God has entrusted to each one of us. © Compass – **Navigating Your Finances God's Way**.

"If you hold to my teaching, you are really my disciples. Then you will know the truth, and the truth will set you free."

John 8:32

Module 1:
"Everything in the heavens and earth is yours, O Lord, and this is your kingdom. We adore you as being in control of everything. Riches and honour come from you alone, and you are the ruler of all mankind; your hand controls power and might, and it is at your discretion that men are made great and given strength." 1 Chronicles 29:11-12 (TLB)

Module 2:
"And God is able to make all grace abound to you, so that in all things at all times, having all that you need, you will abound in every good work." 2 Corinthians 9:8

Module 3:
"The rich rule over the poor and the borrower is servant to the lender." Proverbs 22:7

Module 4:
"Remember this: Whoever sows sparingly will also reap sparingly, and whoever sows generously will also reap generously. Each man should give what he has decided in his heart to give, not reluctantly or under compulsion, for God loves a cheerful giver." 2 Corinthians 9 : 6-7

Module 5:
"The plans of the diligent lead to profit as surely as haste leads to poverty."
"In the house of the wise are stores of choice food and oil, but a foolish man devours all he has."
Proverbs 21:5 and 20

Owner
or manager

Note: If you did not have time to write all these down the fill in text may be found on the last page

The Bible has:

[about]..........................verses on **prayer**, [about] ....verses on **faith**, [about]..........................

verses directly on **money** and [about]..........................verses on the handling of **money** and **possessions**

and [about]..........................verses about **giving** to the **poor**. ....of Christ's written words

were about money and possessions.

Foundation Truth on Money and Possessions. The 2350 verses - free download
Please visit our website - www.yourmoneycounts.org to download your **free copy.** You will find this
in Downloads - Foundation Truth on Money and Possessions.

SCRIPTURE MEMORY VERSE

"Everything in the heavens and earth is yours, O Lord, and this is your kingdom. We adore you as
being in control of everything. Riches and honour come from you alone, and you are the ruler of
all mankind; your hand controls power and might, and it is at your discretion that men are made
great and given strength."

1 Chronicles 29:11-12 (TLB)

BOUGHT

We recommend that before you attend each workshop you
read a few chapters of **Bought**. The relevant part for this
Module is: Part 1: An introduction: Issues and problems.

The Bible describes two different responsibilities in dealing with money. God has His responsibilities and we have ours. Managing money biblically is a partnership between God and each one of us. God reserves certain aspects of money management for Himself and delegates many responsibilities to us. A lot of frustration that we undergo in managing our finances stems from the fact that we do not realise how these responsibilities are divided, what we should do and what only God can do. We will learn more about God's responsibilities and then check to make sure we allow Him to carry these out. Then we will look at the obligations that God delegates to us. In understanding this we can start managing our finances God's way and then we will experience greater financial peace and freedom.

We shall see that the acknowledgement of God's rights to ownership is fundamental to allowing Jesus Christ to be Lord of our money and possessions. If we truly want to be His disciples, we must be prepared to acknowledge that everything belongs to God. Are you ready to make that transfer? Of course, it's not a legal process but it is an important shift in our heart thinking.

"...any of you who does not give up everything he has cannot be my disciple"(Luke 14:33). If we accept that God owns all we manage, then every spending decision becomes a spiritual decision. We will no longer ask, "Lord what would you have me do with my money?" but "Lord, how do you want me to use your money?"

The word which best describes our part is 'steward' or 'manager.' A steward is the manager of another's possessions. The Lord has given us authority be stewards over His possessions. "You made him ruler over the works of your hands;

you put everything under his feet" (Psalm 8:6).

Our responsibility can be summarised in this statement, "Now it is required that those who have been given a trust must prove faithful" (1 Corinthians 4:2). We must, of course, know what is expected of us before any measure of faithfulness can be applied. Just as we consult the manufacturers guide when we buy a new piece of equipment in order to learn how to use it well, so we also study the Bible – the user's manual of the Creator, Owner and Operator, to learn how we can use our money in the most effective way.

"No one can serve two masters. Either he will hate the one and love the other, or he will be devoted to the one and despise the other. You cannot serve both God and Money" (Matthew 6:24). The original word Jesus used in this statement was not mere money, but 'mammon' which depicts the force behind money. He used a word out of the Aramaic language which is a play on words. 'M'aman' means something like 'in whom I trust.' Jesus was warning us that we have to choose between serving God or trusting in money, behind which is a power which is doing its best to compete for our allegiance.

Most people would acknowledge that money has power; purchasing power, power to motivate people and power to enslave people. Trusting in money to provide what we want out of life is commonplace. Living in financial freedom is not a matter of learning some money management techniques, although these are important. It is a matter of being delivered from a spiritual power and living in dependence on God.

Jesus said, "If you hold to my teaching, you are really my disciples. Then you will know the truth, and the truth will set you free" (John 8:32).

Part 1:
The Lord is the owner of all and I am his faithful steward

"Everything in the heavens and earth is yours, O Lord, and this is your kingdom. We adore you as being in control of everything. Riches and honour come from you alone, and you are the ruler of all mankind; your hand controls power and might, and it is at your discretion that men are made great and given strength." 1 Chronicles 29:11-12 (TLB)

God not only created everything, but he has retained the ownership of everything. God still has the title of owner. Psalm 24: 1 and 1 Corinthians 10:26 both tell us the earth is the Lord's.

"You are not your own; you were **Bought** at a price. Therefore honour God with your body." 1 Corinthians 6:19-20

"You intended to harm me, but God intended it for good to accomplish what is now being done, the saving of many lives." Genesis 50:20

...even through difficult circumstances.

"Fear the LORD, you his saints, for those who fear Him lack nothing. The lions may grow weak and hungry, but those who seek the LORD lack no good thing." Psalm 34:9-10

"Again, it will be like a man going on a journey, who called his servants and entrusted his property to them. To one he gave five talents of money, to another two talents, and to another one talent, each according to his ability. Then he went on his journey." Matthew 25:14-15

Capacity = ability & faithfulness

I AM HIS STEWARD (AKA MANAGER)

6. HE ENTRUSTS ME WITH HIS WORK

"When I consider your heavens, the work of your fingers, the moon and the stars, which you have set in place, what is man that you are mindful of him, the son of man that you care for him? You made him a little lower than the heavenly beings and compassed him with glory and honour. You made him ruler over the works of your hands; you put everything under his feet." Psalm 8:3-6

7. HE GIVES US THE ABILITY TO PRODUCE WEALTH

"You may say to yourself not, 'My power and the strength of my hands have produced this wealth for me.' But remember the Lord your God, for it is he who gives you the ability to produce wealth." Deuteronomy 8: 17-18

8. FAITHFULNESS IS ESSENTIAL

"Whoever can be trusted with very little can also be trusted with much, and whoever is dishonest with very little will also be dishonest with much. So if you have not been trustworthy in handling worldly wealth, who will trust you with true riches? And if you have not been trustworthy with someone else's property, who will give you property of your own?" Luke 16:10-12

9. HOW DOES GOD USE MONEY IN MY LIFE?

....

....

....

....

To encourage us to become ....

...., and

....

Note: If you did not have time to write all these down the fill in text may be found on the last page.

10. I AM A STEWARD

Stewardship is not another word for 'giving.' Stewardship is the act of managing wisely the resources entrusted to us by another.

A **Steward** is the one who has been designated to manage someone else's possessions.
Realising that I am a steward gives a new perspective on possessions, work, character, giving and spending.

Let's compare some aspects of **stewardship** with two other common perspectives on money and possessions – the **poverty** perspective and the **prosperity** perspective.

	Poverty	**Prosperity**	**Stewardship**
Possessions are	Evil	A right	A responsibility
I work to	Meet basic needs	Become rich	Serve Christ
Godly people are	Poor	Rich	Faithful
Ungodly people are	Rich	Poor	Unfaithful
I give	Because I must	To get	Because I love God
My spending is	Without joy	Consumptive and carefree	Prayerful and responsible

A RELATIONSHIP WITH MONEY DEFINED

There are four different ways that people relate to money and possessions...

The **self absorbed owner** believes that everything belongs to him and he has full authority in deciding how to use it.

The **obligated owner** believes he owns it all and has full authority over it, but at the same time feels an obligation to give some of his money away.

The **obedient owner** takes seriously the biblical call to tithe 10 per cent to God's work...and usually feels good about being obedient. However, he still retains ownership of the remaining 90 per cent and exercises full authority of what remains 'his'.

The **love-inspired steward** believes deeply that God not only created and provided all that he has, but that the Master retains full ownership. As a result, all decisions related to money and possessions are in the context of seeking God's direction in the use of His possessions.

SELF-ABSORBED OWNER

100% Mine

"I have full authority over my stuff."

OBLIGATED OWNER

£   £

100% Mine

£   £

"I have full authority over my stuff...
but I feel obligated to give something."

OBEDIENT OWNER

God's 10%

90% Mine

"I will obey what God says I should
do with my stuff."

LOVE-INSPIRED STEWARD

100% God's

"I have given God total authority
over His stuff."

Part 2:
The power of mammon

---

1. JESUS GIVES US A DECISION TO MAKE

"No one can serve two masters. Either he will hate the one and love the other, or he will be devoted to the one and despise the other. You cannot serve both God and Money." Matthew 6:24

The original Aramaic word which Jesus used is mammon. Jesus is unmasking a power behind money which he called mammon.

2. WHO IS MAMMON?

= "máman – my trust." Matthew 6:24 and Luke 16:13 (same verse - different gospels)

- A spiritual power
- Creeps unnoticed into our daily lives
- Runs the world's economy
- Competes for our allegiance
- Tries to get us to slip up
- Debt is an important tool
- Has been conquered

3. MAMMON'S PROMISES

Mammon makes empty promises:

- "I will give you..........................."   Matt. 6:19-20
- "I will give you..........................."   Ecclesiastes 5:10-11
- "I will..........................for you"   Psalm 135:15-17
- "I will..........................to you"   Job 31:24
- "I will give you..........................."   Matt 6:25

Note: If you did not have time to write all these down the fill in text may be found on the last page.

1.   Worry and anxiety

2.   Financial disorder – mismanaging money

3.   Structural financial deficit

4.   "I can't afford it" mentality

5.   Impulse purchasing

6.   Stinginess – lack of generosity

7.   Greed

8.   Discontentment

9.   Over indebtedness

10. Overestimating the power of money

De-throne it

- Recognise God's victory
- Recognise God's provision

De-sacralise it

- By giving
- By bringing grace into the world – choose relationships over money

De-part from it

- Avoid debt
- Learn contentment and thankfulness

 LET'S TALK

How do you observe the power of money in:

- your life
- in your workplace/business?
- in the economy?

How can I live victoriously over mammon?

Am I managing money or... is money managing me?

Part 3:
Application

The application section of each of these Modules is for you to complete in your own time.

1.   WHAT IS MY CURRENT FINANCIAL POSITION?

Why create a personal financial overview?

- A snapshot of your assets and liabilities
- A picture of your financial health
- To see where improvement is needed
- To show creditors, if necessary
- To know what you could sell, if necessary (or desirable)

Refer to and complete your own Personal Financial Overview – page 17

2.   HAVE I CONSCIOUSLY TRANSFERRED ALL TO GOD AND ACCEPTED THE
     ASSIGNMENT OF A MANAGER OF GOD'S ASSETS?

"But who am I, and who are my people, that we should be able to give as generously as this? Everything comes from you, and we have given you only what comes from your hand."
1 Chronicles 29:14

"In the same way, any of you who does not give up everything he has cannot be my disciple."
Luke 14:33

Listing your assets and then declaring that they belong to God is one step to acknowledging that everything belongs to God.

Refer to page 18 "Deed of Ownership"

This asks you to list what you "own" and then sign as a key stage in acknowledging that everything belongs to God. If you have never been aware of this before; how does that feel? If you already recognise this - how has your understanding impacted the handling of money and possessions?

MODULE 1

PERSONAL FINANCIAL OVERVIEW

Assets

Possessions – current market value

Short term assets

Can be used in the coming five years

	£
Cash	
Current account	
Savings	
Investments	
Car	
Valuable personal goods	
Other investments	

Short term assets - A

Long term assets

House estimated market value	
Valuation business	
Current value life insurance	
Other real estate	
Pension value	
Other	

Long term assets - C

My total assets - E (A+C)

Liabilities

What I owe – current debt situation

Short term liabilities

Must be paid in the coming five years

	£
Credit card debt	
Current account	
Unpaid bills	
Student loan	
Car loan	
Bank loan	
Other	

Short term liabilities - B

Long term liabilities

House mortgage	
Others	

Long term liabilities - D

My total liabilities - F (B+D)

How are your assets divided between long- and short term?

Short term net value

Short term assets - A

Less: short term debts - B

Long term net value

Long term assets - C

Less: long term debts - D

Total net value: (E-F)

DEED OF OWNERSHIP

DATE: ....

FROM: .... (name + partner's name)

TO: The Lord Jesus Christ

I (we) transfer ownership of the following possessions to the Lord Jesus Christ and thankfully accept the role of manager of these assets. I will faithfully use them according to the Owner's instructions.

SIGNED: Manager(s) of the Lord's possessions:

(1)..

(2)..

Note: This is not a legally binding document. It may take 3 or more months before the heart and mind are aligned with fully recognising that God owns everything.

Extra time

_____

 ACTION

Make sure you have downloaded the 2350 verses on money and possessions from yourmoneycounts.org - Free Resources-downloads

 JOIN US AT THE COFFEE SHOP

Visit www.yourmoneycounts.org.uk - Free Resources - Teaching Videos for a further opportunity to view the coffee shop discussions related to this Module.

 STEWARDSHIP STUDIES: BIBLICAL INSIGHTS

The Faithful Widow - Mark 12: 41-44

MONEY REVEALS OUR TRUE PRIORITIES

One of the major stewardship themes in the Bible is that money reveals our true priorities. Money represents a number of things, but one of the most powerful roles that money plays is in clearly showing us our true priorities. These are revealed not so much in what we say but in what we do. The faithful widow of Mark 12 is a perfect example of this.

 GOING DEEPER

Here are a few additional verses that will help to deepen your understanding of what the Bible has to say about finances.

STEWARDSHIP

> 1 Corinthians 4:2
>
> Matthew 25:15; 19-21
>
> Jeremiah 32:17
>
> Luke 12:25-34

PROVISION

Psalm 35:27

Joshua 1:8

Proverbs 3:9-10

Luke 12:15

1 Kings 17:4-6

Philippians 4:19

Matthew 6:33

 MATERIALISM QUIZ

1. Do you find yourself setting your goals based on achieving a certain financial status or accumulating certain possessions (house, car etc)?

2. Do you almost never seem to have enough time for your family because you have to spend so much time at work?

3. Do you find yourself saying "If I could just get to this point financially, I would be satisfied and happy?"

4. Do you find yourself getting into unneeded debt trying to compete with your friends?

Read Ecclesiastes 5:10-14

"Whoever loves money never has enough; whoever loves wealth is never satisfied with their income. This too is meaningless. As goods increase, so do those who consume them. And what benefit are they to the owners except to feast their eyes on them? The sleep of a labourer is sweet, whether they eat little or much, but as for the rich, their abundance permits them no sleep. I have seen a grievous evil under the sun: wealth hoarded to the harm of its owners, or wealth lost through some misfortune, so that when they have children there is nothing left for them to inherit."

Q: What do you think these verses say about a person who is materialistic?

The Bible tells us that contentment is being satisfied with where we are and what we have because of who we are in Christ.

Society says: "God plays no role in handling money, and my happiness is based on my being able to afford my standard of living."

But, it is impossible to be truly satisfied with material possessions. We will always want more and always be disappointed because the material possessions that we attain don't bring the satisfaction that we thought they would. That is because God is the only one that can give us lasting satisfaction and contentment.

 YOUR THOUGHTS, REFLECTIONS, COMMITMENTS AND ACTIONS

2

Living in
financial freedom

OWNER OR MANAGER

What did we learn?

What was of interest?

Other comments or questions?

SCRIPTURE MEMORY VERSE

"And God is able to make all grace abound to you, so that in all things at all times, having all that you need, you will abound in every good work."

2 Corinthians 9:8

BOUGHT

We recommend that before you attend the next
workshop you read a few chapters of **Bought**.
The relevant part for this Module is Part 2. This includes
looking back at ownership and stewardship with
some interesting different insights.

As we have seen in Luke 16:11, God will only give what He calls the 'true riches' to those whom He finds faithful. Faithfulness implies that we acknowledge God as the Source of all we need for a peaceful and fruitful life, and that we don't allow ourselves to be influenced by all that money claims to offer us. When we acknowledge that God wants to richly bless us while giving priority to the Kingdom of God, (Matthew 6:33), then we will use our money to advance the goals of God's Kingdom.

An essential step towards this is 'closing your financial circle.' That entails making a balanced spending plan which will help you each month to answer the question, 'how much is enough?' The answer to this tough question is very personal, is dependent on one's personal circumstances and is determined by making a good analysis of your obligations, needs and wants. These three categories of spending will describe your financial circle. Closing such a circle and not spending more than you have budgeted for, enables you to bless others with your overflow when God is giving you more than you need. God's blessings, be they material or spiritual are not meant to be kept to oneself. If God grants us a financial excess or overflow then this is not meant to be spent on ourselves or to hoard away, but is always meant to see His work grow in others.

To determine the extent of your financial circle, you will need to embark on a journey of discovery. We will make an analysis of your income and expenditure during a period of 30-60 days.

Most of us know how much income we have, but many people do not always realise where the hard earned money goes. Except that it does just that. For this reason, we will set up a 'spending plan' so that we can learn to close our financial circle. In this way, we can learn to better manage our money without our money managing us! We will learn to better serve God instead of serving money with all its temptations. Together with God, in prayer, we can learn to make wise decisions on how to use the money which he has entrusted to us and make money our slave instead of allowing it to be our master. God has an opinion on how we are to design our spending plan. The way we spend our money is an outward sign of our inward priorities. Mammon would have us grow in consumerism and have us think that we are the boss over our spending.

Living without a budget is living with an 'open circle'. When our income increases, the circle expands with increased spending and there is no overflow for God's purposes. To prevent this, we need to close the circle, say that 'this is enough' and use the overflow for God's purposes.

You will work on building a spending plan during the duration of this course. We will refine it, adapt it and change it. Ask God for His counsel and advice. He wants to be involved in how we use His money. He will help us to carry out a plan, so that we might be found faithful and then He can entrust us with much more; true riches' which will bring us life in abundance (John 10:10).

Part 1:
Living in the circle
of God's blessing

1. THE LORD BLESSES US ...

"He shall live in the circle of God's blessing..." Psalm 25:13 (Living)

Obligations	Needs
Fixed costs	Variable costs

Desires
Periodic

2. A CIRCLE OF GOD'S PROTECTION

"For the LORD your God is God of gods and Lord of lords, the great God, mighty and awesome, who shows no partiality and accepts no bribes. He defends the cause of the fatherless and the widow, and loves the alien, giving him food and clothing." Deuteronomy 10:17-18

3. A CIRCLE OF GOD'S PROVISION

The most High God is our Provider

Consider the lilies of the field...   Matthew 6:25-34
    He clothes them
Consider the sparrows...
    He feeds them

Can we not trust Him for our finances and discuss this with him in prayer?

4. COUNTING THE COST

"Suppose one of you wants to build a tower. Will he not first sit down and estimate the cost to see if he has enough money to complete it? For if he lays the foundation and is not able to finish it, everyone who sees it will ridicule him, saying, 'This fellow began to build and was not able to finish.'" Luke 14:28-30

5. HIS SUPPLY IS ALWAYS ENOUGH

"… and God is able to make all grace abound to you, so that in all things at all times, having all that you need, you will abound in every good work." 2 Corinthians 9:8

We will study how much is enough in Module 5.

6. THIS IS NOT A CIRCLE OF DENIAL

"Delight yourself in the LORD and He will give you the desires of your heart." Psalm 37:4

Have you discussed with God, which desires He will put on your heart to then give you?

7. MONEY IN THE 'JARS'

In generations past people used jars to keep monies separated for different purposes. Some still do this today, while others use envelopes to keep monies planned for a purpose separate so that it is not spent other than that for which it is intended.

Rent – food – clothing – saving

Three principles:
1. Money was assigned to a purpose
2. No money? Then no more spending
3. Knowing what is still left over in the jar

8. AN OPEN CIRCLE

An open circle: spending grows with new wants
More income: no room left to bless others with

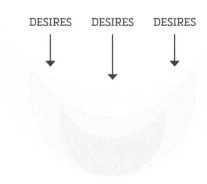

9. A CLOSED CIRCLE

The circle of enough, gives extra money to invest in medium and long term plans and generosity.

"Do not be deceived: God cannot be mocked. A man reaps what he sows. Whoever sows to please their flesh, from the flesh will reap destruction; whoever sows to please the Spirit, from the Spirit will reap eternal life." Galatians 6: 7-8

We simply cannot have it both ways. We will either allow God to be the influence in our lives or we will allow the force of money to be the influence. Following both is not an option. We also are confronted with the reality that how we manage the 'little things' in life, like money, will indicate how we will handle the 'true riches' of God's Kingdom.

 LET'S TALK

Discuss the concepts of a 'closed circle' and an 'open circle.'

Discuss the pressure from society to continuously raise your standard of living.

The challenge for most people is that their earning capacity does not match their yearning capacity.

Anonymous

Part 2:
Living in financial freedom

1.   BE SATISFIED WITH WHAT YOU HAVE

"Keep your lives free from the love of money and be content with what you have, because God has said, "Never will I leave you; never will I forsake you." So we say with confidence, "The Lord is my helper; I will not be afraid. What can man do to me?" Hebrews 13:5-6

2. DO NOT BE CONFORMED TO THE WAYS OF THE WORLD

"Do not conform to the pattern of this world, but be transformed by the renewing of your mind. Then you will be able to test and approve what God's will is—His good, pleasing and perfect will." Romans 12: 2

3.   INDEPENDENT OF CIRCUMSTANCES

"I am not saying this because I am in need, for I have learned to be content whatever the circumstances. I know what it is to be in need, and I know what it is to have plenty. I have learned the secret of being content in any and every situation, whether well fed or hungry, whether living in plenty or in want. I can do everything through him who gives me strength." Philippians 4:11-13

4.   LIVING MORE SIMPLY?

"But whatever was to my profit I now consider loss for the sake of Christ. What is more, I consider everything a loss compared to the surpassing greatness of knowing Christ Jesus my Lord, for whose sake I have lost all things. I consider them rubbish, that I may gain Christ and be found in Him, not having a righteousness of my own that comes from the law, but that which is through faith in Christ—the righteousness that comes from God and is by faith." Philippians 3:7-9

5. TRUST IN GOD NOT IN RICHES

"Command those who are rich in this present world not to be arrogant nor to put their hope in wealth, which is so uncertain, but to put their hope in God, who richly provides us with everything for our enjoyment." 1 Timothy 6:17

6. AVOID THE LOVE OF MONEY

"For the love of money is a root of all kinds of evil. Some people, eager for money, have wandered from the faith and pierced themselves with many griefs." 1 Timothy 6:6-10

7. DELAYED GRATIFICATION

"So I say, live by the Spirit, and you will not gratify the desires of the flesh. For the flesh desires what is contrary to the Spirit, and the Spirit what is contrary to the flesh. They are in conflict with each other, so that you are not to do whatever you want. But if you are led by the Spirit, you are not under the law." Galatians 5:16-18

Where riches hold dominion of the heart God has lost His authority.

John Calvin

Part 3:
Application

The application section of each of these Modules is for you to complete in your own time.

MAKING A FINANCIAL PLAN

1.   MAKING IT TO THE END OF THE MONTH

"Be sure you know the condition of your flocks, give careful attention to your herds; for riches do not endure forever, and a compass is not secure for all generations. When the hay is removed and new growth appears and the grass from the hills is gathered in, the lambs will provide you with clothing, and the goats with the price of a field, you will have plenty of goats' milk to feed you and your family and to nourish your servant girls." Proverbs 27:23-27

2.   MAKE A FINANCIAL PLAN TO MANAGE YOUR MONEY

- Analyse where your money is going
- Put income and expenses in categories
- Make a first spending plan
- Use the plan and update as you change your spending decisions
- Manage your cash flow and save for larger purchases.

3.   ANALYSE WHERE YOUR MONEY IS GOING

- Write down everything you spend
- Over a period that is not less than 30 days
- Divide spending into categories
- Make a preliminary overall plan.

Fixed income	Variable income
Salary	Commission
Child benefit	Bonus
Rent	Tips
Alimony	Business income
Pension	Interest/dividends
Tax relief payments	Other income
Holiday pay	

Obligations	Needs	Wants
Tithes/gifts	Contribution	Clothes
Housing	Subscription	Furnishings
Travel	School	Garden
Insurance	Childcare	Recreation
Debts	Groceries	Holiday
		Car reserve
		Medical expenses
		Saving/investing

Income		Expenditure	
Salary - 1	....	Savings	....
Salary - 2	+	Food	+ ....
Other income	+	Housing	+ ....
Total income:	=	Travel	+ ....
			+ ....
Less: taxes still to pay:	–		+ ....
Less: Giving to God	–	Total expenditure:	= ....
Net spendable income:	=	Income – Expenditure	= ....

7. ADJUST EXPENDITURE

- Compare actual spending with budget
- Which categories of expenses should be adjusted?

Extra time

 JOIN US AT THE COFFEE SHOP

Visit www.yourmoneycounts.org.uk - Free Resources -Teaching Videos for a further chance to view the coffee shop discussions related to this Module.

 STEWARDSHIP STUDIES: BIBLICAL INSIGHTS

The Good Samaritan – Luke 10: 30-37

MONEY INTENDED TO DO GOOD IN GOD'S KINGDOM

Money has a huge role to play in leveraging the good we can do in people's lives. The Good Samaritan had the desire to help, but his willingness to use his resources allowed him to help more effectively.

 GOING DEEPER

WHAT THE BIBLE SAYS ABOUT WEALTH

Deuteronomy 6:10-13	Can dull our spiritual vision
Deuteronomy 8:11-20	Can cause you to forget God
Nehemiah 5:9-11	Taking advantage of others to increase yours
Mark 10:21	Dealing with the love of
Mark 10:23	How it makes one less dependent on God
Luke 12:15	Not the same as the good life
Luke 12:33	Using it wisely
1 Timothy 6	Great chapter to read especially verses 6-10 and 17-19 Possessing much wealth carries greater responsibility
James 1:9-11	What true wealth is
James 2:2-4	Gaining proper perspective of
Revelation 18:4-8	Can make you too comfortable

ARE YOU A SPENDER OR SAVER?

		Always	Often	Sometimes	Rarely	Never
1	When I do my food shop I buy whatever takes my fancy	1	2	3	4	5
2	I love to buy myself a treat at the end of a hard day	1	2	3	4	5
3	I have spare cash in my purse/wallet	5	4	3	2	1
4	I borrow from my friends and family	1	2	3	4	5
5	I love to work on my budget, making tweaks where needed	5	4	3	2	1
6	Impulse buying is a weakness of mine	1	2	3	4	5
7	I prefer to stay at home in the evenings so that I don't spend any money	5	4	3	2	1
8	I find it hard to keep paying off my credit card	1	2	3	4	5
9	I make sure I have a voucher when I go out for a meal	5	4	3	2	1
10	I only spend money that I've saved, it feels very satisfying	5	4	3	2	1
11	Once I start shopping I just can't stop	1	2	3	4	5
12	I have multiple store cards	1	2	3	4	5
13	If I got a bonus at work, I would spend it straight away	1	2	3	4	5
14	I feel satisfied when I see my bank balance grow	5	4	3	2	1
15	I feel that it's worth spending my money on luxury items	1	2	3	4	5
16	I find it difficult to spend on people when Christmas comes around	5	4	3	2	1
17	I love shopping in second-hand shops, you can find real bargains	5	4	3	2	1
18	I only buy something when I know I need it	5	4	3	2	1
19	Money is there for me to bring happiness to myself and others	1	2	3	4	5
20	I make sure that I have savings for my long-term future	5	4	3	2	1

APPLICATION - RESULTS

1-20   Spend-a-Lot: You love spending your money on things quickly and often spontaneously. Be careful to spend within your means. Spontaneity isn't a bad thing, as long as you have a fund set aside for spontaneous spending!

21-40   On the Spending Side: You usually succumb to "impulse buys" but here is a part of you that sometimes stops you before you hand the money over.

41-60   Good Balance: You are planned but your planning restricts you from making quick financial decisions. Just make sure you stick to your budget and you'll be fine.

61-80   On the Saving Side: You enjoy seeing those savings build up and would rather sacrifice short-term gain for your long-term plan. You sometimes act spontaneously, so factor this in when building your budget.

81-100 Super-Saver: You love to save every penny. It's great to be wise with your money but don't limit your generosity or stop yourself enjoying your life whilst you save.

3

Free
to serve

What did we learn?

What was of interest?

Other comments or questions?

SCRIPTURE MEMORY VERSE

"The rich rule over the poor and the borrower is servant/slave to the lender."

Proverbs 22:7

BOUGHT

We recommend that before you attend the next workshop
you read a few chapters of **Bought**. The relevant part
for this Module is: Part 3: Free to serve Him

Many of us have allowed ourselves to get into so much debt that the man (or woman) in the street is described as one who drives on the roads which are financed through government bonds, in a car owned by the bank with fuel paid by credit card, on the way to buy furniture in easy installments for a house financed by a mortgage to impress people we don't like. The bumper sticker with the line, "The one who dies with most toys wins" is a sad reality for many people.

The dictionary describes debt as: "money which we are obliged to pay back." Debt encompasses money owed to credit card companies, bank loans, money borrowed from family members, mortgage and unpaid bills. Invoices to be expected such as the monthly energy bill are not considered debt when paid on time. It is important to realise the real cost of credit card debt.

Please study the following table. This seeks to highlight the alarming cost of owing money to card companies and contrasts this with the meagre returns for those saving. Charging an interest rate of 18 per cent on a constant card debt of **£5,555** the interest cost is **£1,000** a year.

The table contrasts what the **lender earns** from that **£1,000** interest a year with their 18 per cent return and compares what the **saver earns** at 2 per cent when saving £1,000 a year. There is a difference and it is larger than perhaps you would think! The chart seeks to show the impact at the end of a 40 year period.

The desire for money is an addiction.
Spending is a therapy.

Philip Bishop

Scenario:

One person (A) saves [monthly £83.33] **£1,000** a year for 40 years and ends up saving **£40,000** of their own money at the end of 40 years.

Another person (B) owes the credit card company a constant debt of **£5,555** for 40 years (i.e. they only pay interest so that the debt remains the same) and the interest @ 18% each year will be **£1,000** [monthly £83.33]. So, in this case there is **£40,000** paid out in credit card interest.

The **saver** earns **2%** per annum [compounded] on their savings
The credit card holder pays **18%** per annum on the credit card debt

The difference appears to be 9x (2 compared to 18%) but is that really the case?

	Saver has	Credit card company has
Interest **earned** by **A** at 2% at the end of 40 years	£21,200	
Interest **earned** by the **credit card company** at 18% over the 40 years on the £40,000	£	

How much more does that 18% earn the card company?

Does that make the credit card company profit model somewhat [anagram] D C W K E I: ....

A 25-year home mortgage, at an annual interest rate of 5% on a repayment basis to the mortgage will require you to pay more than 75 per cent more than the amount originally borrowed.

Original mortgage amount	£120,000
Monthly mortgage payment at 5 per cent (APR-5.12%)	£702
Months paid	300 (25 years)
Total paid	£210,529
Total interest paid	£90,529
Interest cost compared to the original loan	75%

Debt can also extract a physical toll. It often increases stress, which contributes to mental, physical and emotional fatigue. It can stifle creativity and harm relationships. Many people raise their standard of living through debt, only to discover that the burden of debt controls their lifestyles. The car sticker that reads "I owe, I owe, it's off to work I go," is an unfortunate reality for too many people.

Up-to-date debt statistics can be found on themoneycharity.org.uk website.

Part 1:
What does the Bible say?

1. OWE NO-ONE ANYTHING

"Let no debt remain outstanding, except the continuing debt to love one another, for he who loves his fellow man has fulfilled the law." Romans 13:8

What does debt have to do with love?

2. DEBT ROBS YOU OF YOUR FREEDOM

"The rich rule over the poor, and the borrower is servant to the lender." Proverbs 22:7

3. IN THE OLD TESTAMENT – DEBT OFTEN AROSE AS A RESULT OF DISOBEDIENCE

"The alien who lives among you will rise above you higher and higher, but you will sink lower and lower. He will lend to you, but you will not lend to him. He will be the head, but you will be the tail." Deuteronomy 28:43-44

4. IN THE OLD TESTAMENT FREEDOM CAME AS A RESULT OF OBEDIENCE

"All these blessings will come upon you and accompany you if you obey the LORD your God: The LORD will open the heavens, the storehouse of his bounty, to send rain on your land in season and to bless all the work of your hands. You will lend to many nations but will borrow from none." Deuteronomy 28:2, 12

5. DEBT PRESUMES ON THE FUTURE

"Now listen, you who say, "Today or tomorrow we will go to this or that city, spend a year there, carry on business and make money." Why, you do not even know what will happen tomorrow. What is your life? You are a mist that appears for a little while and then vanishes. Instead, you ought to say, "If it is the Lord's will, we will live and do this or that." As it is, you boast and brag. All such boasting is evil. Anyone, then, who knows the good he ought to do and doesn't do it, sins." James 4:13-16

6. DEBT CAN BE A HINDRANCE TO GOD PROVIDING

"For my thoughts are not your thoughts, neither are your ways my ways," declares the LORD. "As the heavens are higher than the earth, so are my ways higher than your ways and my thoughts than your thoughts." Isaiah 55:8-9

Could God provide in another way, if you are short of money to purchase something?

7. NOT PAYING BACK COMPARED TO SIN

"The wicked borrow and do not repay, but the righteous give generously." Psalm 37:21

Is there a difference between debt and borrowing?

8. WHAT THE BIBLE HAS TO SAY ABOUT CO-SIGNING

"Do not be a man who strikes hands in pledge or puts up security for debts; if you lack the means to pay, your very bed will be snatched from under you." Proverbs 22:26-27

9. DON'T JEOPARDISE THE FAMILY

"If anyone does not provide for his relatives, and especially for his immediate family, he has denied the faith and is worse than an unbeliever." 1 Timothy 5:8

Be careful, very careful about allowing your house to be used as security for lending. It is not just a house, it is a home.

10. WATCH OUT FOR YOUR MOTIVES

"Then Jesus said to them, "Watch out! Be on your guard against all kinds of greed; a man's life does not consist in the abundance of his possessions." Luke 12:15

Part 2:
Borrowing principles

Every Bible reference to debt is always in the negative - warning of the dangers of debt. But the Bible is silent regarding when debt might be incurred. So, the Your Money Counts guideline is that debt may be considered for three types of debt:

1. An asset that increases in value

2. Investing in education

3. Investing in a business.

But please ensure that you seek advice / wise counsel.

1. CAN I PAY BACK?

"This is also why you pay taxes, for the authorities are God's servants, who give their full time to governing. Give to everyone what you owe them: if you owe taxes, pay taxes; if revenue, then revenue; if respect, then respect; if honour, then honour." Romans 13:6-7

Also please refer to Luke 14: 28-30, Proverbs 21:5.

2. DOES IT MAKE ECONOMIC SENSE?

Is the return from the loan greater than the cost?

Will the value of the purchase increase over time?

Never borrow for consumptive purposes.

3. DO WE HAVE PEACE ABOUT IT?

"Let the peace of Christ rule in your hearts, since as members of one body you were called to peace. And be thankful." Colossians 3:15

Do you have the 'peace of mind that passes all understanding?'

Rule = let peace of mind be a key determining factor

Which are 'God-given' goals?

Is there really no other way than incurring debt?

"Everything is permissible for me"—but not everything is beneficial. "Everything is permissible for me"—but I will not be mastered by anything." 1 Corinthians 6:12

Psychological factors?

- Maximum financial flexibility
- The least possible limitations

Important point: Give yourself margin and do not borrow up to the hilt. How would you repay if your income reduced or ceased?

"The wife of a man from the company of the prophets cried out to Elisha, "Your servant my husband is dead, and you know that he revered the LORD. But now his creditor is coming to take my two boys as his slaves." Elisha replied to her, "How can I help you? Tell me, what do you have in your house?" "Your servant has nothing there at all," she said, "except a little oil." Elisha said, "Go around and ask all your neighbors for empty jars. Don't ask for just a few. Then go inside and shut the door behind you and your sons. Pour oil into all the jars, and as each is filled, put it to one side." She left him and afterward shut the door behind her and her sons. They brought the jars to her and she kept pouring. When all the jars were full, she said to her son, "Bring me another one." But he replied, "There is not a jar left." Then the oil stopped flowing. She went and told the man of God, and he said, "Go, sell the oil and pay your debts. You and your sons can live on what is left." 2 Kings 4: 1-7

Six key steps:
1. Go to the Lord...
2. Use what you.. have
3. Borrow...
4. Close the...
5. Trust...
6. Live from God's...

Note: If you did not have time to write all these down the fill in text may be found on the last page.

Part 3:
Application

The application section of each of these Modules is for you to complete in your own time.

Spending can so easily become an addiction and the consequence for so many is...debt. So, the habit of spending needs to be broken in order to loose the chains and bondage of debt.

SEEK TO BE DEBT FREE

"Free yourself, like a gazelle from the hand of the hunter, like a bird from the snare of the fowler." Proverbs 6:5

EIGHT STEPS TO BECOMING DEBT-FREE

1. Pray
2. Enter into no new debts - not one penny more!
3. Make a list of all your debts
4. Use a written plan to control your expenses
5. Make a debt repayment plan
6. Reduce your expenses
7. Can you increase your income?
8. Should you seek a debt buddy?

STEP 1: PRAY

"Do not be anxious about anything, but in everything, by prayer and petition, with thanksgiving, present your requests to God." Philippians 4:6

What to pray?

1. Transfer ....
2. ....
3. ....
4. ....
5. Ask for ....

Note: If you did not have time to write all these down the fill in text may be found on the last page.

STEP 2: ENTER INTO NO NEW DEBTS

"A prudent man sees danger and takes refuge, but the simple keep going and suffer for it." Proverbs 22:3

Action?

1. Enter ....

2. Plastic ....

3. Use ....

4. Use ....

5. NO ....

Note: If you did not have time to write all these down the fill in text may be found on the last page.

STEP 3: MAKE A LIST OF ALL YOUR DEBTS

Creditor	Amount	Monthly payments	Number of outstanding payments	Interest	Notes

STEP 4: USE A BUDGET

- Spend less than you earn
- Set aside a sum of money to use to accelerate debt repayments (in the example below we have found another £150 to pay off the debts)

STEP 5: MAKE A DEBT REPAYMENT PLAN

- Communicate with your creditors, make an agreement and honour it
- Use the 'snowball method'

Monthly Payments Applying the Snowball System

Creditor	Debt	Interest	Min. month. payments	Extra payment. £150	After 3 months	After 6 months	After 15 months	After 22 months	After 26 months
Mail order	£372	18%	£15	£165	paid				
Dad	£550	0	£20	£20	£185	paid			
Bank (overdraft)	£1,980	19%	£40	£40	£40	£225	paid		
Pers. Loan	£2,369	16.9%	£50	£50	£50	£50	£275	paid	
Car	£7,200	6.9%	£259	£259	£259	£259	£259	£534	paid
Total	£12,471		£384	£534	£534	£534	£534	£534	

Note: After all is paid off, you have £534 each month left over.

STEP 6: HOW CAN YOU REDUCE YOUR EXPENSES?

- To build up a reserve/savings account for future expenditures
- 3-6 months living expenses
- Cash for large purchases

STEP 7: SEEK TO INCREASE YOUR INCOME

- Part-time job?
- Something to sell?
- Use extra tax relief or bonuses to reduce debt

STEP 8: WOULD IT HELP TO HAVE A DEBT BUDDY?

- Someone you know who has experience and wisdom
- A debt agency

"For lack of guidance a nation falls, but victory is won through many advisors." Proverbs 11:14

"The way of fools seems right to them, but the wise listen to advice." Proverbs 12:15

LET'S TALK

Extra time

GET MORE INSIGHTS AT
→ WWW.YOURMONEYCOUNTS.ORG.UK

 JOIN US AT THE COFFEE SHOP

Visit www.yourmoneycounts.org.uk - Free Resources -Teaching Videos for a further chance to view the coffee shop discussions related to this Module.

 STEWARDSHIP STUDIES: BIBLICAL INSIGHTS

The rich and the kingdom of God – Luke 18: 18-23

OUR ATTACHMENT TO MONEY IS A "TEST" OF OUR DESIRE FOR CHRIST

We are told that money is a test. As in the case of the Rich Young Ruler we also are tested by having to choose between following Jesus and following money and wealth. The Rich Young Ruler desired to be with Jesus, but his desire to hang onto his wealth was stronger. When tested by Jesus...he failed with disastrous consequences!

 PARENTS

Teaching your children about managing the money that passes through their hands and how they manage cards and the easy invitation to swipe and buy is important. We will look further at this in a later Module but for now you might like to look at our Parent Money Management Questionnaire.

PARENT MONEY MANAGEMENT QUESTIONNAIRE

This questionnaire is designed to help parents focus on some of the aspects of money education for your children. There is no right or wrong answer. The purpose of the questions is to stir up your thinking about certain attitudes and behaviour. The questions relate to two specific areas of financial concern: your children's money and their possessions.

1. I consistently give into my child's demands for more things, whether I think he or she has earned them or not.

2. I give my child a regular allowance and allow him or her to decide how to budget and spend it.

3. My child's room is filled almost to overflowing with toys and other fun things, largely because my neighbour's children have the same.

4. I periodically require my child to list and evaluate his or her possessions to determine their present practicality and usefulness.

Good parenting tip. Teach your children what the Bible says about the handling of money and possessions. Show and practice the ways of the Lord (Proverbs 22:6) before the world teaches them (how to spend, spend, oh and borrow as well).

Under 7s   – Give Save Spend

8-12s   – The Secret

Order copies of these books from: www.yourmoneycounts.org.uk/shop

DEBT STRESS TEST

1. Is your debt making your home life unhappy?   Yes/No

2. Does the pressure of your debts distract you from your daily work?   Yes/No

3. Are your debts affecting your reputation?   Yes/No

4. Do your debts cause you to think less of yourself?   Yes/No

5. Have you ever given false information in order to obtain credit?   Yes/No

6. Does the pressure of your debts make you careless in the welfare of your family?   Yes/No

7. Do you ever fear that your employer, family or friends will learn the extent of your total indebtedness? Yes/No

8. Does the pressure of your debts ever cause you to have difficulty sleeping?   Yes/No

9. Have you ever borrowed money without giving adequate consideration to the rate of interest you are required to pay?   Yes/No

10. Have you ever developed a strict plan for paying off your debts, only to break it under pressure?   Yes/No

IN PSALM 31 WE LEARN MORE ABOUT HOW THE LORD WILL DIRECT YOUR JOURNEY WHEN YOU ALLOW HIM TO BE YOUR SPIRITUAL GPS

God's Protection System (vs1, 20-23)
God's Protection System is better, more thorough and less expensive monetarily than those offered by any home security systems

God's Power System (vs 2)
God hasn't left us powerless

God's Positioning System (vs 3-5)
God is asking us the same question today. He wants to know where you are in fulfilling His purposes for your life, your calling, and the goals He's directed you to achieve.

God's Peace System (vs 7)
The Lord will give you His strength and peace in the midst of every adversity

God's Possibility System (vs 14)
It doesn't matter how many times you may have failed in life. . .rise up and get started again

God's Promotion System (vs 15-19)
Your promotion comes from the Lord. He gives you the power and favour for advancement in every single area of human endeavour

God's Prosperity System (Joshua 1:8)
Joshua 1:8 in the Amplified Bible says: "This Book of the Law shall not depart out of your mouth, but you shall meditate on it day and night, that you may observe and do according to all that is written in it. For then you shall make your way prosperous, and then you shall deal wisely and have good success."
2 Chronicles 26:5 tell us that so "long as he sought the LORD, God made him to prosper."

4

Growing
in generosity

What did we learn?

What was of interest?

Other comments or questions?

SCRIPTURE MEMORY VERSE

"Remember this: Whoever sows sparingly will also reap sparingly, and whoever sows generously will also reap generously. Each man should give what he has decided in his heart to give, not reluctantly or under compulsion, for God loves a cheerful giver."

2 Corinthians 9 : 6-7

BOUGHT

We recommend that before you attend the next workshop
you read a few chapters of **Bought**. The relevant part for
this Module is: Part 4: Growing in generosity.

Generous living is learning to live as a child of the great Giver. This entails being generous in all He has given to us and learning to be content with what he has given to us, knowing that He will provide all we need.

Giving blesses the receiver, the Church can carry out its commission, the hungry are fed, the poor receive clothing and missionaries and mission trips can serve the Lord's purposes. However, in God's economy, generosity with the right heart attitude can bring even more blessings to the giver. "Remembering the words the Lord Jesus himself said: 'It is more blessed to give than to receive' " (Acts 20:35).

The apostle Paul wrote in 1 Timothy 6:8: "But if we have food and clothing, we will be content with that." If this was an advert, it could sound like this: "if you can afford the best food, the most beautiful and latest fashion and the most luxurious house, then you will be happy." Our society is based on the presupposition that 'more is better' and that happiness and contentment is based on being able to increase our possessions.

The word 'contentment 'can be found seven times in the Bible and always is connected to money. Paul wrote, "I have learned to be content whatever the circumstances. I know what it is to be in need, and I know what it is to have plenty. I have learned the secret of being content in any and every situation, whether well fed or hungry, whether living in plenty or in want. I can do everything through him who gives me strength" (Philippians 4:11-13). Paul 'learned' to be content. We are not born content. It is something to be leaned. The secret of contentment has three elements, as illustrated in the figure below:

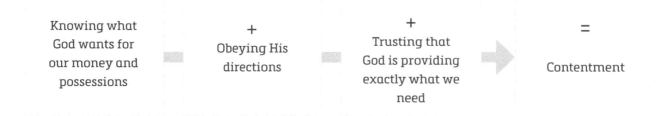

| Knowing what God wants for our money and possessions | + Obeying His directions | + Trusting that God is providing exactly what we need | = Contentment |

If I live out of a conviction that 'God is the Owner, and I am His faithful servant', when I enter into a conversation with Him about how to use the things He has entrusted to me, and live an adjusted lifestyle, then I have a foundation for true contentment. Then I have acknowledged that everything I have in life is actually a gift from God. That makes me thankful, and then, out of a attitude of thankfulness, I can serve God and my neighbour with all my heart.

Part 1:
Growing in generosity

1. GENEROSITY IS TANGIBLE EVIDENCE OF OUR LOVE FOR GOD

"They gave themselves first of all to the Lord, and then by the will of God also to us." 2 Corinthians 8:5

2. GIVING BRINGS JOY

"Now I commit you to God and to the word of his grace, which can build you up and give you an inheritance among all those who are sanctified. I have not coveted anyone's silver or gold or clothing. You yourselves know that these hands of mine have supplied my own needs and the needs of my companions. In everything I did, I showed you that by this kind of hard work we must help the weak, remembering the words the Lord Jesus himself said: 'It is more blessed to give than to receive.'" Acts 20:32-34

3. GENEROSITY HONOURS THE LORD

"What is more, he was chosen by the churches to accompany us as we carry the offering, which we administer in order to honour the Lord himself and to show our eagerness to help."
2 Corinthians 8:19

4. GIVE FROM WHATEVER YOU ALREADY HAVE …

"And now, brothers, we want you to know about the grace that God has given the Macedonian churches. Out of the most severe trial, their overflowing joy and their extreme poverty welled up in rich generosity. For I testify that they gave as much as they were able, and even beyond their ability." 2 Corinthians 8:1-3

5. PRINCIPLES OF PLANNING FOR GENEROUS GIVING

Priority – personal and proportionate

"On the first day of every week, each one of you should set aside a sum of money in keeping with his income…" 1 Corinthians 16:2

Percentage

"His stone that I have set up as a pillar will be God's house, and of all that you give me I will give you a tenth." Genesis 28:22

10 per cent is a great place to start.

Premeditated

"Each of you should give what you have decided in your heart to give, not reluctantly or under compulsion, for God loves a cheerful giver." 2 Corinthians 9:7

...and cheerfully!

6. THREE LEVELS OF GIVING

Level	Biblical term	Process	Reason
Should give	Tithe	Percentage and priority	Response to God's ownership
Could give	Offerings	Planning	Desiring to be a disciple
Would want to give	Faith	Promise	Exercise faith and experience God

7. THERE ARE FIVE TYPES OF GIVING:

1. ....

2. ....

3. ....

4. ....

5. ....

8. PLANNING FOR WHEN GOD BLESSES YOU

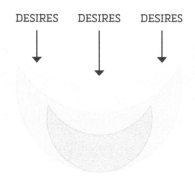

DESIRES   DESIRES   DESIRES

Can you find new friends?

Stewardship, generosity, and giving are sometimes [incorrectly] used interchangeably.

Stewardship is the act of managing what does not really belong to us. Generosity is a willingness to sacrifice for the benefit of others and giving is an act of releasing something of value. This could be time and talents as well as treasure.

Stewardship: The act of managing wisely 'God's stuff' to please the Master.

- **Generosity:** A willingness to share with others. . . that involves personal sacrifice.
- **Giving:** The act of releasing something of value in one's possession.

What does this verse mean and how how do you see this verse applying today?

"Do not lay up for yourselves treasures on earth, where moth and rust destroy and where thieves break in and steal, but lay up for yourselves treasures in heaven, where neither moth nor rust destroys and where thieves do not break in and steal. For where your treasure is, there your heart will be also." Matthew 6:18-20

*You are never more like Jesus than
when you are giving.*

Johnny Hunt, First Baptist, Woodstock, GA, USA

Part 2:
Contentment and enjoyment

1. CONTENTMENT IS AN ART

"Now this is what the LORD Almighty says: "Give careful thought to your ways. You have planted much, but have harvested little. You eat, but never have enough. You drink, but never have your fill. You put on clothes, but are not warm. You earn wages, only to put them in a purse with holes in it. This is what the LORD Almighty says: "Give careful thought to your ways." Haggai 1:5-7

2. CONTENTMENT IS GOOD FOR YOU

"A heart at peace gives life to the body, but envy rots the bones." Proverbs 14:30

3. CONTENTMENT DOES NOT COME FROM MONEY

"Keep your lives free from the love of money and be content with what you have, because God has said, 'Never will I leave you; never will I forsake you.'" Hebrews 13:5

Read also Philippians 4: 11-13 and Ecclesiastes 5: 10-12.

4. CONTENTMENT IS FINDING A BALANCE

"Two things I ask of you, O LORD; do not refuse me before I die: Keep falsehood and lies far from me; give me neither poverty nor riches, but give me only my daily bread. Otherwise, I may have too much and disown you and say, 'Who is the LORD? 'Or I may become poor and steal, and so dishonour the name of my God." Proverbs 30:8-9

5. ENJOY WHAT YOU HAVE

"Moreover, when God gives any man wealth and possessions, and enables him to enjoy them, to accept his lot and be happy in his work—this is a gift of God." Ecclesiastes 5:19

6. FOUR THIEVES OF JOY

"The thief comes only to steal and kill and destroy; I have come that they may have life, and have it to the full." John 10:10

- Fear
  "Therefore I tell you, do not worry about your life, what you will eat or drink; or about your body, what you will wear. Is not life more than food, and the body more than clothes?... But seek first His kingdom and his righteousness, and all these things will be given to you as well." Matthew 6:25,33

- Comparing
  "Keep your lives free from the love of money and be content with what you have, because God has said, 'Never will I leave you; never will I forsake you.' " Hebrews 13:5

- Greed
  "Those who want to get rich fall into temptation and a trap and into many foolish and harmful desires that plunge people into ruin and destruction. For the love of money is a root of all kinds of evil. Some people, eager for money, have wandered from the faith and pierced themselves with many griefs." 1 Timothy 6:9-10

- False guilt
  "Command those who are rich in this present world not to be arrogant nor to put their hope in wealth, which is so uncertain, but to put their hope in God, who richly provides us with everything for our enjoyment." 1 Timothy 6:17

 LET'S TALK

Discuss the question: How much is enough?

To what extent do you experience peer pressure in the workplace or your family?

What do you desire?

Part 3:
Application

The application section of each of these Modules is for you to complete in your own time.

1.   GROWING IN GENEROSITY

With a prayer that the Lord will help us to grow in generosity, in faith, we make the following plan...

Faith giving plan	Amount
Each month we will set this aside	
As an offer, we could give, saving on the following expenses	
What we would like to give if God blesses us with overflow	

2.   WHERE COULD I SAVE MONEY?

	Annual savings - £	Yield in 10 years at 3% Interest - £
Choose a smaller car	2,000	23,289
Spend less on holiday	1,000	11,644
Discipline in shopping	1,200	13,974
Stop smoking; or any other 'unnecessary' habits	1,500	17,467
Stop with sweets/choc/cake etc	800	9,315
Stop with national lottery	156	1,816
Totals	**6,656**	**77,505**

3.   ADJUST YOUR PERSONAL BUDGET

Here is an example. On the next page is an empty table for your own use. Pray about each category.

Budget adjustments of: John and Mary Smith   Date: 31 March 2020

Sample budget adjustments

Category	Adjustments	Expected amount £
1. Tithing and gifts	We want to set aside each month 10% for the Lord on a separate account	475 per month
2. Taxes	Reserve £50 a month for expected extra taxes	50 per month
3. Housing	Research to see if we can find a cheaper mortgage	Unknown
4. Food and housekeeping	Reduce our spending at the supermarket	46 per month
5. Transport	Carpool to work	60 per month
6. Insurances	Get quotes from other companies	Unknown
7. Debts		
8. Entertainment & recreation	One less evening eating out	75 per month
9. Clothes	Need to increase budget - underestimated	50 per month
10. Savings	Decided to save £100 each month	
11. Medical		
12. Diverse	Second TV subscription stop	21 per month
13. Investments		
14. School		

Budget adjustments of: ....   Date: ....

Your actual budget adjustments

Category	Adjustments	Expected amount £
1. Tithing and gifts		
2. Taxes		
3. Housing		
4. Food and housekeeping		
5. Transport		
6. Insurances		
7. Debts		
8. Entertainment & recreation		
9. Clothes		
10. Savings		
11. Medical		
12. Diverse		
13. Investments		
14. School		

4.   ADJUST YOUR SPENDING PLAN

Estimated spending plan

Budget

Monthly income				Less:		
Salary (-ies)						
Travel expenses						
Interest income (bank)						
Tax refunds						
Holiday pay						
Children's allowance				1. Giving, charitable donations	£	
Other				2. Other taxes	£	
Total monthly income	£			**Net spendable income NSI**	£	

Fixed expenses		Variable costs	
3. Home	£	9. Housekeeping/living	£
Mortgage/rent		Food, supermarket	
Service costs, leasing		Washing, cleaning	
Insurances		Cosmetics, toiletries	
Rates		Hair care	
Waste removal		Others	
Electricity		10. Clothes and shoes	£
Gas			
Water		**Fixed + variable costs**	£
Telephone/Internet/CableTV			
Others			
4. Transport	£	**Periodic costs**	
Replacement, payments		11. Furniture, house equipment	£
Oil and gas		12. Maintenance home, garden	£
Insurance		13. Medical costs	£
Licenses/taxes		14. Recreation, holiday	£
Maintenance		15. Saving and investing	£
Others			
5. Insurances	£	**Total cost of living (Items 3-15)**	£
Life insurance			
Health insurance		**Income minus costs**	
Liability insurance		Net spendable income	£
Others		Less: total cost of living	£
6. Debts	£		
Loans		**Excess or deficit**	£
7. Subscriptions	£		
Newspapers, magazines		Balance excluding savings	£
Sport etc.			
8. School costs	£		
Childcare			
Study costs, books			

Extra time

JOIN US AT THE COFFEE SHOP

Visit www.yourmoneycounts.org.uk - Free Resources -Teaching Videos for a further chance to view the coffee shop discussions related to this Module.

STEWARDSHIP STUDIES: BIBLICAL INSIGHTS

Stewardship is about our hearts – Mark 14: 3-9

WE NEED TO GUARD OUR HEART ATTITUDES

It can be easy to assume that stewardship is about our efforts to support good causes in the name of Christ. Clearly there is nothing wrong with supporting worthy Kingdom causes, but Jesus emphasised that true stewardship is an attitude of the heart and not an action to be undertaken. Mary's love for Jesus resulted in overwhelming generosity and sacrifice focused on Him. Yet the disciples criticised her for not using her wealth to support the poor while Jesus commended her devotion and love.

GOING DEEPER

NEW TESTAMENT GUIDELINES FOR GIVING: GIVE, CHRISTIAN GIVE

There are no exceptions. "Each man should give what he has decided in his head to give." 2 Corinthians 9:7

Mark 14:3-9	Give generously
1 Corinthians 16:2 2 Corinthians 8:8-11	Give regularly and systematically - generosity is tangible evidence of our love for God
2 Corinthians 8:4; 9:7	Give voluntarily - generosity cannot be contained
2 Corinthians 8:2 Acts 20:35 Matthew 6:21	Give joyfully - giving is unrelated to income and wealth
Acts 10:1-4 2 Corinthians 8:9 Matthew 25:40 Matthew 5:23, 24	Give worshipfully

Acts 11:29 1 Corinthians 16:2 Mark 12:43-44	Give proportionately
2 Corinthians 8:3 Luke 21:1-4 2 Samuel 24:24	Give sacrificially - giving is never forced
Matthew 6:1-4	Give quietly
2 Corinthians 8:5	Generosity is always focused first toward the Lord
2 Corinthians 8:14	Generous people meet needs
2 Corinthians 8:19	Generosity honours the Lord
2 Corinthians 9:7	True generosity is expressed cheerfully and is personal between the giver and God

THE LORD'S PROVISION FOR THE GIVER

In Proverbs 11:24-25 and in Luke 6:38, the Bible makes it clear that in many cases God blesses us financially when we give generously and in 2 Corinthians 9:6, God reminds us that the sower who sows little or no seed will receive little or possibly none. However, the sower who sows generously will reap generously. God prospers us not just so we can have more ourselves, but that we can give even more to those who are in need. 2 Corinthians 9:11 – God's extra provision is usually not intended to raise our standard of living but to raise our standard of giving.

QUESTIONS ABOUT GIVING?

WHY SHOULD I GIVE?

- Give because you love God (Matthew 22:37-38)
- Give because you love others (Matthew 22:39-40)
- Give because you desire God's blessing on your life (Luke 6:38 and John 15:9-12)

YOUR THOUGHTS, REFLECTIONS, COMMITMENTS AND ACTIONS

5

Saving
and investing

What did we learn?

What was of interest?

Other comments or questions?

SCRIPTURE MEMORY VERSES

"The plans of the diligent lead to profit as surely as haste leads to poverty."

"In the house of the wise are stores of choice food and oil, but a foolish man devours all he has."

Proverbs 21:5 and 20

BOUGHT

We recommend that before you attend the final workshop you read a few chapters of **Bought**. The relevant part for this Module is: Part 5: Save. Invest. Spend.

In 1 Timothy 6:10 we read "For the love of money is a root of all kinds of evil. Some people, eager for money, have wandered from the faith and pierced themselves with many griefs."

It is not money, but the love of money, a wrong attitude towards money which is at the root of all kinds of evil. In the Old Testament we read about the lives of many wealthy people, such as Job, Abraham and David, but they didn't allow their wealth to get in the way of a rich relationship with God.

Matthew 6:19-21, would appear to give the impression that Jesus is against saving and investing is: "Do not store up for yourselves treasures on earth, where moth and rust destroy, and where thieves break in and steal. But store up for yourselves treasures in heaven, where moth and rust do not destroy, and where thieves do not break in and steal. For where your treasure is, there your heart will be also."

Jesus explains this further in a parable of a rich man who stored up riches for himself. Luke 12:16-21, 34: "And he told them this parable: "The ground of a certain rich man produced a good crop. He thought to himself, 'What shall I do? I have no place to store my crops .'Then he said, 'This is what I'll do. I will tear down my barns and build bigger ones, and there I will store all my grain and my goods. And I'll say to myself, "You have plenty of good things laid up for many years. Take life easy; eat, drink and be merry." "But God said to him, 'You fool! This very night your life will be demanded from you. Then who will get what you have prepared for yourself?' "This is how it will be with anyone who stores up things for himself but is not rich toward God.".. For where your treasure is, there your heart will be also."

The key word in this story is 'all'. Jesus called the rich man a fool because he stored and saved all his goods. He stored all for himself. There was no balance between the need to save and the need to be a generous giver. It is only safe to store and save if we are also giving to the One who provided all in the first place. Why? Because of Jesus' teaching that where your treasure is, there your heart will be also. If we only concentrate on saving and investing, our attention will be solely focused on those. But if we bring our saving and investing in balance with investing in the purposes of the Owner of all, then, we can ensure that God receives the focus of our attention.

Prior to designing an investment strategy, it is important to set financial goals. The very first step in building up an investment portfolio is very simple. Ensure you are spending less than you earn, do this over a long period of time and invest the savings with a long-term strategy. Unfortunately, many people live from hand-to-mouth, finding it difficult to make it to the end of the month.

The Bible encourages us to save. Solomon the wise King says it like this: "In the house of the wise are stores of choice food and oil, but a foolish man devours all he has." (Proverbs 21:20). We can also turn our attention to the ant for advice on saving for future needs. "Four things on earth are small, yet they are extremely wise: Ants are creatures of little strength, yet they store up their food in the summer" (Proverbs 30:24-25).

Savings are the opposite to borrowings. Saving gives us a certain store for tomorrow's needs. Borrowing is relying on a very uncertain future.

Part 1:
Saving

Setting funds aside from today's income to provide for the time when work is not the first call of duty is important. Let's explore what the Bible has to say about planning for tomorrow.

1. THE BIBLE RECOMMENDS IT

"In the house of the wise are stores of choice food and oil, but a foolish man devours all he has." Proverbs 21:20

2. SAVE, BUT ALL IS TEMPORAL, SO GIVE

"And he told them this parable: "The ground of a certain rich man produced a good crop. He thought to himself, 'What shall I do? I have no place to store my crops.' "Then he said, 'This is what I'll do. I will tear down my barns and build bigger ones, and there I will store all my grain and my goods. And I'll say to myself, "You have plenty of good things laid up for many years. Take life easy; eat, drink and be merry." "But God said to him, 'You fool! This very night your life will be demanded from you. Then who will get what you have prepared for yourself? "This is how it will be with anyone who stores up things for himself but is not rich toward God."... For where your treasure is, there your heart will be also." Luke 12:16-21, 34

3. SAVE REGULARLY, SET GOALS AND MAKE A PLAN

"The plans of the diligent lead to profit as surely as haste leads to poverty." Proverbs 21:5

4. SAVING IS WISE

"And now let Pharaoh look for a discerning and wise man and put him in charge of the land of Egypt. Let Pharaoh appoint commissioners over the land to take a fifth of the harvest of Egypt during the seven years of abundance. They should collect all the food of these good years that are coming and store up the grain under the authority of Pharaoh, to be kept in the cities for food. This food should be held in reserve for the country, to be used during the seven years of famine that will come upon Egypt, so that the country may not be ruined by the famine." Genesis 41:33-36

5. SAVING IS SENSIBLE

"Go to the ant, you sluggard; consider its ways and be wise! It has no commander, no overseer or ruler, yet it stores its provisions in summer and gathers its food at harvest." Proverbs 6:6-8

6. WHAT IS YOUR MOTIVE FOR SAVING?

"People who want to get rich fall into temptation and a trap and into many foolish and harmful desires that plunge men into ruin and destruction. For the love of money is a root of all kinds of evil. Some people, eager for money, have wandered from the faith and pierced themselves with many griefs."
1 Timothy 6:9-10

7. WHICH TREASURE IS IMPORTANT?

"Do not store up for yourselves treasures on earth, where moth and rust destroy, and where thieves break in and steal. But store up for yourselves treasures in heaven, where moth and rust do not destroy, and where thieves do not break in and steal. For where your treasure is, there your heart will be also."
Matthew 6:19-21

8. DON'T LET YOUR FOCUS BE DISTURBED BY MAMMON

"The eye is the lamp of the body. If your eyes are good, your whole body will be full of light. But if your eyes are bad, your whole body will be full of darkness. If then the light within you is darkness, how great is that darkness." Matthew 6:22-23

 LET'S TALK

Discuss an example whereby your focus could be blurred by mammon

How would you determine the balance between saving and spending?

What savings goals do you set?

Part 2:
Investing

1. HOW MUCH IS ENOUGH?

"Whoever loves money never has enough; whoever loves wealth is never satisfied with their income. This too is meaningless. As goods increase, so do those who consume them. And what benefit are they to the owners except to feast their eyes on them? The sleep of a labourer is sweet, whether they eat little or much, but as for the rich, their abundance permits them no sleep." Ecclesiastes 5:10-12

2. TEN BIBLICAL PRINCIPLES ABOUT INVESTING

1. Set up ....financial goals — Proverbs 20:5; 21:5
2. Seek ....counsel — Proverbs: 20:18
3. Develop a .... perspective — Luke 14:28
4. .... your portfolio — Ecclesiastes 11:2
5. Avoid a '.......................................' attitude, grow slow — Proverbs 28:20,22
6. Avoid .... investments if you cannot afford to lose — Ecclesiastes 5:13-15
7. Avoid too high .... — Proverbs 22:7
8. Beware of .... — Psalm 131:1
9. .... your total investment — Proverbs 15:16; 30:8
10. Share and discuss decisions with your .... — Genesis 2:24

Note: If you did not have time to write all these down the fill in text may be found on the last page.

3. THE PROCESS OF FINANCIAL PLANNING

Vision	Strategy	Investment results
Values + expected	Discipline + wisdom	(rewards)

4. THE PROCESS OF FINANCIAL PLANNING TO ACHIEVE LONG TERM GOALS

1. Analyse your situation

2. Set financial goals

3. Set priorities

4. Manage the cash flow. Control spending. Minimise impulse expenditure.

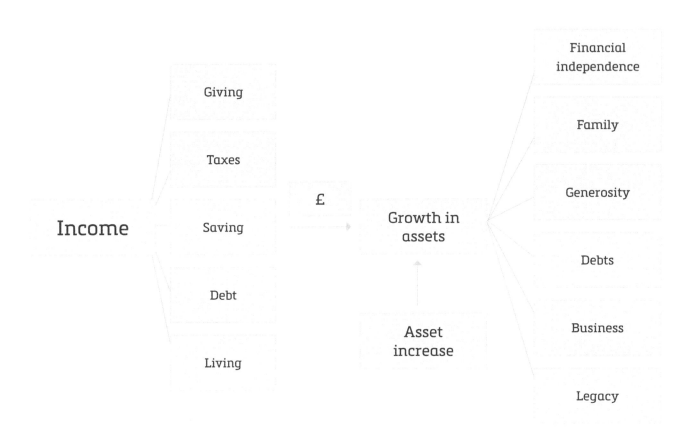

5. INSURANCE GUIDELINES

Practical Principle 1: Trust God's provision
Matt 6: 25-34

Practical Principle 2: Care for the family
1 Timothy 5:8

Practical Principle 3: Take obligatory insurance
Romans 13:1-7

Practical Principle 4: Insure only those risks you cannot wisely carry yourself

Practical Principle 5: Seek competitive quotes but beware of using companies you have never heard of.

Part 3:
Application

The application section of each of these Modules is for you to complete in your own time.

1. SAVING AND INVESTING

Shorter	Time frame	Longer
Cash or cash equivalent	Bonds/fixed interest	Shared (equities) /property
Investments easily converted to cash	Issued by a lender seeking to raise funds	Ownership of company shares/property
Interest bearing deposits	Bond funds	Equity funds
		Individual shares
Cash ISA	Government bonds (gilts)	Property

Lower ◄———————— Risk and return ————————► Higher

INVESTING PRINCIPLES

When deciding where to invest, you need to consider your goals, time frame and tolerance to risk. The concept of risk is important because, as the time and risk diagram shows, investments with the best track record also carry the greatest potential for loss – at least in the short term.

In other words, the more time you have, the more you can afford to invest in assets such as shares (also called equities) or property either directly or via a 'collective investment' or 'fund'. These are all the type of investments that can lose value in the short term but historically, have produced the best returns over the long term. If you have 5, 10 or 20 years before you need the money, you can probably recover from most market downturns; but if you need it in less than five, you will need to adapt your strategy to match this shorter term perspective.

A study of investment returns since 1891 shows that equities have outperformed cash deposits in 75% of consecutive 5 year periods and in 93% of consecutive 10 year periods. Although history might not repeat itself, equities are usually held in the hope of getting a better return than cash and it is generally accepted that equity investments should be held with a minimum of a 5-year time horizon.

This means using varying investments for different goals with different time frames. An investment that is suitable for a 15-year goal is simply not appropriate for money you will need in two years. If you need the deposit to buy your home in two years as opposed to funding your retirement in 15 years, you will invest the money differently, moving your money into more conservative investments as you get closer to the time you will need to spend it.

Here are strategies to consider over the short (less than five years) and long (more than five years) term.

If you need the money in less than five years (or in the case of your emergency fund, might need the money at short notice), you should consider investing in cash or in what is sometimes referred to as 'cash equivalents' e.g. fixed rate current accounts, certain national savings and investment (NS&I) products or a cash ISA.

Bank/building society accounts

You can sometimes obtain a better rate of interest by investing for a fixed period (e.g. 1 to 3 years) or accepting a longer 'notice period' (e.g. 30 to 90 days) instead of immediate access or by opting for an account operated by post or the Internet.

It is important to review savings accounts regularly. Banks will often offer a competitive rate of interest to attract savers and then gradually reduce it, leaving unwary customers in accounts with low interest.

If the bank were to go into liquidation, the Financial Services Compensation Scheme provides protection up to a certain amount.

National savings and investments (NS&I)

NS&I provide greater security than a bank because they are backed by the government although they do not usually offer rates of interest that are as high as the most competitive bank and building society accounts. A number of NS&I products are not subject to income tax although the returns are lower to account for this.

In times of higher inflation (or if you are concerned about higher inflation in the future), National Savings Index Linked Certificates, provide a small return plus inflation (measured by RPI) and are free of income tax and are worth considering.

The most common investments for longer than five years are bonds, shares and property, often using collective investment funds.

Shares/equities

When you buy a share, you are purchasing part of a company. Generally shares have one of the greatest opportunities for profit, but you can also lose a lot if the company does not perform well.

Some shares also provide a small stream of income through a dividend.

Bonds

When you buy a bond, you loan money to a business or the government, and they pay you interest. Investors buy government bonds for safety; and corporate bonds for higher yields. It is important to realise that when interest rates rise, the value of bonds decline, and vice versa.

There is also the risk of loss if the bond issuer defaults, for example in the case of a corporate bond, the company goes into liquidation.

Property

People buy property for income and capital appreciation. However, unlike publicly traded stocks, shares or bonds that can be sold quickly, property may require a long time to sell. Buy-to-let properties have been a popular form of investment for many, although tax rules now make buy to let investments far less attractive.

While these may provide long term capital appreciation, care must be exercised in order to avoid the danger of loan repayments exceeding rental income if interest rates rise. Also, there should be adequate cash reserves to provide for loan repayments and other costs if there is a period when the property is unoccupied. Investing in buy-to-let property does require time as well as money, and care needs to be taken to comply with letting regulations and such issues as health and safety rules. It is best considered as a business rather than just an investment.

There are also a number of 'alternative' investments such as commodities, hedge funds, fine wine, works of art etc. that are specialist areas. You should seek specialist advice if you are thinking of investing in one of these.

Collective investments

A collective investment is usually a fund where investors' money is pooled together and managed by an investment company. This allows a small investor to gain access to a much larger spread of investments than would be possible by purchasing individual shares, bonds or properties. Using a collective investment, means that the risk of loss through one company doing badly (or gaining if one company does well) is significantly reduced.

There are many types of collective investments with different legal structures such as unit trusts, open ended investment companies (OEICs) (sometimes called mutual funds), exchange traded funds (ETFs), investment trusts, life insurance funds and pension funds.

There are collective investments for different types of investments. For example, some funds are composed of shares, others of bonds. Others consist of international shares or are limited in their selection to an investment, such as property or shares in a particular foreign stock market.

A balanced fund invests in a range of different asset classes, usually cash, bonds and shares. Some balanced funds use commodities or hedge-funds in an attempt to reduce risk by providing further diversification from traditional asset classes such as shares and bonds.

ALLOCATING YOUR INVESTMENTS

Asset allocation is the term given to deciding how much to invest in shares, property, fixed interest and cash etc. Within an asset class there might be further asset allocation decisions e.g. how much to allocate to UK and overseas equities.

There are several academic studies indicating that in the long term, asset allocation is the main factor in explaining both the risk and returns of an investment portfolio.

The most appropriate asset allocation for you will depend on your goals, time frame and attitude to investment risk. Always maintain a foundation of conservative investments for short term contingencies as this provides a stable base on which to build.

Short term: up to five years

As outlined above, this should be largely cash based.

Medium term: 6-15 years

A conservative mix of investments with approximately 50 per cent in cash and bonds and 50 per cent in shares depending on your attitude to risk, income requirements and goals might be appropriate. A more conservative approach would be to reduce the amount in shares to say 30% to 40%. A more speculative approach might increase the shares to 60% or 70%.

Long term: over 15 years

Higher risk funds e.g. 60 per cent to 80 per cent in shares depending on your attitude to risk, income requirements and goals. A more conservative investor, may still use a 50:50 or more cautious approach with longer term funds although there is the risk in the long term that the value of cash or fixed interest investments can be eroded by inflation.

Your goals

All of the above depends on your own goals as well as your attitude to investment risk. For example, a young person saving regularly for retirement can afford to take greater investment risk in the early years because they do not have so much to lose if investments fall in value. Once they are older, and have built up a pension fund they will be more concerned with preserving capital and, in due course, providing an income from that capital. They may therefore wish to be more conservative as their time horizon reduces and they have 'more to lose'.

TAXATION CONSIDERATIONS

Income tax is normally paid on bank or bond interest, rental income from a property and dividends from a share. Capital gains tax may be payable if an investment such as a share or property is sold at a profit.

There are a number of 'structures' (sometimes called 'tax wrappers') that reduce or delay the levying for income tax or capital gains tax. These include individual savings accounts (ISAs), pensions, life insurance policies, venture capital trusts (VCTs) and enterprise zone trusts (EZTs).

7. DO YOU HAVE AN UP-TO-DATE WILL?

A WILL

1.   May serve as a person's final testimony

2.   Only controls property belonging to the person whose Will it is

3.   Is a legal document that directs how property will be passed to family members, friends, relatives and charitable organisations after the death

4.   Authorises payment of debts and expenses owed

5.   Does not control property that goes to others by legal devices such as jointly held property or beneficiaries

6. May nominate a person to serve as legal guardian to minor children and other persons to whom the deceased person has custodial responsibility

7. Names an Executor/Executrix who will see that all provisions of the document are carried out

8. May be amended by a codicil any time during the maker's life

9. Is only effective when the maker is deceased

10. Needs to be valid and up-to-date, both from the standpoint of your wishes and legislation, which may change. So, check your Will every two or three years

11. A Will may be subject to amendment through a deed of variation for up to two years after death provided the beneficiaries affected agree.

TIPS FOR WILL PREPARATION FOR CHRISTIANS

1. Start with prayer...that God will guide you, and that He will reveal His will for your Will.

2. Help your solicitor prepare your Will.... The following is a summary of information you should consider, and your solicitor will need, in order to prepare your Will. It addresses your concerns and desires for how you want your assets distributed when you die. Many of these issues should be discussed with your legal advisor, or another person and prayed about before a meeting. Thinking through these matters will reduce the time and money you will spend on this service.

3. Gather and record pertinent information about your estate as this will help you think and pray through how you wish to deal with your estate. We recommend you provide your solicitor with a personal financial statement form.* This will give you a better idea of the size and components of your estate. You may decide that your estate is of a size and complexity that

you should seek outside estate planning advice in order to take advantage of available tax and charitable tax deductions. Or you may wish to ask your solicitor about establishing a trust.

4. As you work through the details, write down questions you wish to ask your solicitor. At some point during the process, you probably will want to discuss your desires and your plans with your adult children or other beneficiaries.

5. If you are going to make a bequest to a Christian organisation or charity, it is helpful to notify that organisation of your intention...but not necessarily the amount.

6. What about a solicitor? Most solicitors can prepare a Will. However, if you can find a Christian solicitor, it may be to your advantage. Ask your pastor or a close friend to recommend someone in your area.

7. You will want to review your Will every two or three years as circumstances change in your life and in the lives of those to whom you have made bequests (marriages, births, deaths, financial gains or losses, personal or spiritual goals).

8. After the Will is prepared, leave a copy with your solicitor. Put another copy in a safe place in your home where it is accessible. You may want to give it to your executor.

DEATH IS ONE APPOINTMENT NONE OF US WILL MISS

Death comes to all us in the end, regardless of whether we have made a Will, have you thought about making a Will but never got round to it, or have never let it cross your mind? If you do have a valid Will at the time of your death you will die intestate and the intestacy rules determine who inherits what.

*These notes do not represent financial advice. It is important to seek proper financial advice.

3. INSURANCE EXAMPLES

Insurance type	Annual premium	Insurer	Broker	Action to take: Keep, stop, shop around, change, self-insure etc.
Home				
Fire				
Contents				
Life				
Health				
Partner				
Life				
Income				
Funeral				
Transport				
Car - 1				
Car - 2				
Motorcycle				
Others				
Travel				
Pets				
Caravan/boat				
Liability				
Legal				
Business				
Others				

4. MY LIFE GOALS

Determining your life goals at the end of this Module will help you accomplish what is important to you. Here's how to proceed:

1. Complete the following my life goals worksheet. If you are married, we recommend that you and your spouse individually write down your financial goals on separate sheets of paper. Then compare goals and compile a complete list on the my life goals worksheet.

2. List your goals for the coming year. One caution: do not set unrealistic goals. It's better to accomplish three goals than to become frustrated with 10 unattainable ones.

Matt and Jennifer's goals reflect their plans to live a life according to their Christian beliefs, this is evidenced in particular, in their goals for volunteering work and lifestyle aspirations.

MY LIFE GOALS SAMPLE – 1

Date: January 2020   Matt and Jennifer

Giving goals

Would like to give   11% of my income

Would like to increase my giving by   1   per cent each year

Other giving goals   Give £1,000 over the next five years to our
                                      church's Food for the Poor team

Debt repayment goals

Would like to pay off the following debts first:

Creditor	Amount
Debenhams	£100
VISA	£900
Spring Finance	£4,000

Educational goals

Would like to fund the following education:

Person	School	Annual cost	Total cost
John	Local college	£5,000	£15,000
Ruth	University	£4,000	£32,000

Lifestyle goals

Would like to make these major purchases: (home, car, travel, appliances)

Item	Cost
Add conservatory to home	£8,000
Replace Jennifer's car	£7,500
Upgrade to large fridge freezer	£1,000

Would like to achieve an income of   £45,000 p.a.

MY LIFE GOALS SAMPLE – 1

Date: ....

Giving goals

Would like to give

Would like to increase my giving by   per cent each year

Other giving goals

Debt repayment goals

Would like to pay off the following debts first:

Creditor	Amount

Educational goals

Would like to fund the following education:

Person	School	Annual cost	Total cost

Lifestyle goals

Would like to make these major purchases: (home, car, travel, appliances)

Item	Cost

Would like to achieve an income of

MY LIFE GOALS SAMPLE – 2

Date: January 2020   Matt and Jennifer

Savings and investment goals

Would like to save   6   per cent of my income

Other savings goals: Increase savings to 12% a year within 10 years

Would like to make the following investments: Amount

    Pension Account   £2,000 each year

    ISA   £2,000 each year

Would like to provide my/our heirs with the following: House and adequate insurance to provide them with capital to repay their debts and income to fund our grandchildren's education.

Starting a business

Would like to invest in or begin my/our own business: Matt would like to own a car dealership within the next 10 years.

Describe your standard of living that you sense would please the Lord:

We would be satisfied living in our present home (not moving to a larger or more expensive one). We have the goal of adding a conservatory to our home. We want to concentrate on educating our children, paying off debts, giving more and saving, rather than increasing our standard of living for the next 15 years. After we have accomplished our financial goals, we want to travel once a year and give away fifteen per cent of our income. We would like to keep our cars an average of seven years and purchase low-mileage used cars. We want to maintain a simple and more classic wardrobe rather than following clothing fads. We also want to help our children purchase their first home. We want everything we spend to please the Lord.

MY LIFE GOALS SAMPLE – 2

Date: ....

Savings and investment goals

Would like to save   per cent of my income

Other savings goals:

Would like to make the following investments: Amount

Would like to provide my/our heirs with the following:

Starting a business

Would like to invest in or begin my/our own business:

Describe your standard of living that you sense would please the Lord:

MY LIFE GOALS SAMPLE - 3

Date: January 2020   Matt and Jennifer

Volunteer/ministry goals

Would like to volunteer to help in the church toddler nursery for eight weeks

Would like to volunteer two hours a week as a Group Leader

Would like to volunteer to help with the Food for the Poor Team

Financial goals for this year

I believe the Lord wants me/us to achieve the following goals this year

Priority	Financial goals	God's part	Our part
1	Increase giving	Provide money	Write cheque
2	Balance spending plan	Give wisdom	Reduce spending
3	Pay off credit card	Provide buyer for bike	Sell bike
4	Pay off furniture loan	Provide money	Increase income
5			
6			
7			
8			
9			
10			

MY LIFE GOALS SAMPLE – 3

Date: ....

Volunteer/ministry goals

Financial goals for this year

I believe the Lord wants me/us to achieve the following goals this year

Priority	Financial goals	God's part	Our part
1			
2			
3			
4			
5			
6			
7			
8			
9			
10			

CHRISTIAN PERSPECTIVE:

Pray for the Lord to confirm your goals. Do not limit yourself by your present circumstances. Remember the division of financial responsibilities: Our part and God's part. Our part is to do what we can as faithful stewards; God's part is to meet our needs and dispense possessions as He sees fit. Many of your goals may be 'faith goals' that you must trust the Lord to provide. Then prioritise your goals. For instance, funding education might be more important than buying a second car. Also, you don't have to accomplish all your goals at once. For example, your spending plan may not allow you to save as much as you want.

There are two times in a man's life when he should not speculate; when he can't afford it, and when he can.

Mark Twain, American author

Extra
time

___

JOIN US AT THE COFFEE SHOP

Visit www.yourmoneycounts.org.uk - Free Resources -Teaching Videos for a further chance to view the coffee shop discussions related to this Module.

STEWARDSHIP STUDIES: BIBLICAL INSIGHTS

**Our tithe is an acknowledgement of being under a higher spiritual authority –
Genesis 14: 18-20 and Hebrews 7**

Our sincere tithing is motivated by both practical and spiritual reasons. One of the most powerful, yet often overlooked, is the understanding that the first example of the tithe in Genesis 14 involves Abraham tithing to the priest Melchizedek. Melchizedek represented for Abraham a greater spiritual authority in his life. His tithe was a tangible gesture to acknowledge that fact.

GOING DEEPER

BOUGHT

We recommend that after studying **Navigating Your Finances God's Way** you read the final chapter in **Bought**: Part 6: Summing it all up.

As this is your own personal study book why not prepare a record of all that you have learnt. The decisions and commitments you have made. Applying biblical financial principles is a journey that takes time. It's easy to become discouraged when your finances aren't completely under control by the end of this Module. It takes the average person a year to apply most of these principles, and even longer if you have made financial mistakes.

Some people become frustrated by the inability to solve their financial problems quickly. Remember simply be faithful with what you have – be it little or much. Some abandon the goal of becoming debt-free or increasing their saving or giving because the task looks impossible. And perhaps it is – without the Lord's help. Your role is to make a genuine effort, no matter how small it may appear, and then leave the results to God. I love what the Lord said to the prophet Zechariah, "For who has despised the day of small things" (Zechariah 4:10). Don't be discouraged. Be persistent. Be faithful in even the smallest matters. We have repeatedly seen the Lord bless those who tried to be faithful.

We appreciate the effort you have invested in this study. And we pray this has given you a greater appreciation for the Bible, helped close friendships, and above all, nurtured your love for Jesus Christ. May the Lord richly bless you on your journey to true financial freedom.

REGULAR TEACHING UPDATES

If you have downloaded the 2350 verses you will automatically receive our monthly Teaching Update. If not, please visit our site to register for our Monthly Blog (Teaching Update). We look forward to being in touch with you.

Notes

If you were unable to complete the blanks in the manual here is what they are:

MODULE 1 INTRODUCTION

The Bible has:

[about] 500 verses on prayer, [about] 500 verses on faith, but [about] 700 verses directly on money and [about] 2350 verses the handling of money and possessions and [about] 300 verses about giving to the poor. 15 per cent of Christ's written words were about money and possessions.

MODULE 1 - PART 1

8. How does God use money in my life?

To test my faithfulness

To teach satisfaction

To develop unity

To give assignments

Independent from the world, and

Dependent on God

MODULE 1 - PART 2

3. Mammon's empty promises

I will give you security	Matt. 6:19-20
I will give you satisfaction	Ecclesiastes 5:10-11
I will provide for you	Psalm 135:15-17
I will talk to you	Job 31:24
I will give you peace	Matt 6:25

MODULE 3 - PART 2

Go to the Lord first

Use what you already have

Borrow wisely

Close the circle

Trust God

Live from God's provision

MODULE 3 - PART 3

Step 1:

What to pray?

1. Transfer ownership
2. Confess
3. Promise
4. Obedience
5. Ask for help

Step 2:

1. Enter into no new debts
2. Plastic surgery
3. Use cash
4. Use envelope system
5. No CONsolidation loans

MODULE 4 - PART 1

There are five types of giving

1. Invisible money
2. Pocket money
3. Wallet or purse money
4. Current account money
5. Serious money

MODULE 5 - PART 2

1. Set up written financial goals
Proverbs 20:5; 21:5

2. Seek wise counsel
Proverbs: 20:18

3. Develop a long-term perspective
Luke 14:28

4. Diversify your portfolio
Ecclesiastes 11:2

5. Avoid a 'get-rich-quick' attitude, grow slow
Proverbs 28:20,22

6. Avoid risky investments if you cannot afford to lose
Ecclesiastes 5:13-15

7. Avoid too high leveraging
Proverbs 22:7

8. Beware of anxiety
Psalm 131:1

9. Limit your total investment
Proverbs 15:16; 30:8

10. Share and discuss decisions with your spouse
Genesis 2:24